T0196681

AFRICAN SMALL PUBLISHERS' CATALOGUE

2021

Edited and compiled by
Colleen Higgs & Aimee-Claire Smith

African Small Publishers' Catalogue 2021

First published by Modjaji Books in 2021
www.modjajibooks.co.za
info@modjajibooks.co.za

Editors: Colleen Higgs & Aimee-Claire Smith
Cover design & tyepsetting: Monique Cleghorn
Cover photograph of colourful bracelets © iStockphoto/intek1

ISBN (Print): 978-1-928433-27-9
ISBN (ebook): 978-1-928433-30-9

The printing of this catalogue kindly sponsored by:
XMD BOOKS

CONTENTS

88 CLASSIFIEDS

89 ARTICLES:

INTRODUCTION

This is the fifth edition of the *African Small Publishers' Catalogue*. Once again we have many more publishers and some of the publishers we featured last time have either left the scene, or their circumstances have changed such that they don't want to be included in the catalogue. We are also aware of how challenging the COVID-19 pandemic has been for publishers in Africa.

The catalogue is a showcase of the variety and extent of independent and small publishing in Africa. It is still weighted with many more South African publishers, but each time we have brought out a new edition, there are more publishers from a wider spread of African publishers. This year we have a publisher from Malawi for the first time. We have listings from 21 countries

The catalogue aims to uncover and highlight the work and existence of small publishers in Africa. We hope that librarians, booksellers, books page editors, educators, readers, writers and bigger publishers will be enriched by having access to these publishers and that the publishers themselves will find new customers, access to funds and technologies that will enable them to thrive.

It is thrilling to see all the writers and publishers who are toiling away, doing extraordinary creative cultural work.

EDITORS

Colleen Higgs is a publisher and writer, who lives in
Cape Town. She started Modjaji Books in 2007, and still
works there as the publisher. Her most recent book is a
memoir, *my mother, my madness* (deep south) which came
out in 2020. Higgs is a publishing activist, and this catalogue
is one of the ways she contributes to book development and
raising the profile of independent publishing in Africa.

Aimee-Claire Smith lives in Cape Town, where they are
studying English Literature and Anthropology. They work in
publishing and media. Their writing has been published in
New Contrast, *Living While Feminist* (Kwela, 2020) and
Supernova.

LISTINGS

AERIAL PUBLISHING
SOUTH AFRICA

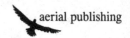

📍 c/o The Institute for the Study of English in Africa,
Rhodes University, Makhanda

✉ PO Box 6082, Makhanda 6140

@ aerial.publishing.grahamstown@gmail.com

📞 +27 46 622 5081

Aerial Publishing is a Grahamstown-based community
publisher, publishing mainly previously unpublished
Eastern Cape poets. It emerged from the popular four
month creative writing course which has been running at
the Rhodes Institute for the Study of English in Africa
(ISEA) since 1998, when writers associated with the course
decided to publish individual collections. As new writers are
published, they are invited to become part of the collective
which selects, edits and publishes the next books. All money
made from sales goes towards the publishing of future titles.
Aerial Publishing's first two poetry collections were
published in 2004 and we're still going strong.

AFRICAN SUN PRESS
SOUTH AFRICA

AFRICAN SUN PRESS
www.afsun.co.za

3 Florida Road, Vredehoek, Cape Town 8001

afpress@iafrica.com

afsun.co.za

+27 21 461 1601; +27 721 844 600 : Patricia Schonstein

We are the leading publisher of poetry anthologies in South Africa, and associates of Poetry in McGregor through whom we present the annual Patricia Schonstein Poetry in McGregor Award. We publish occasional books for children under Seed Readers. We administer the publishing rights of Patricia Schonstein and Don Pinnock and curate the Pinnock Photographic Archive.

AKOOBOOKS LIMITED
GHANA

📍 33 Legon Hill, Accra

✉ P. O. Box 1002, Leggon, Accra

@ ama.dadson@akoobooks.com

🌐 app.akoobooks.net

📞 +233 202040176 : Ama Dadson

ⓕ akoobooks   ⓖ akoobooks

AkooBooks Audio is a platform and African spoken audio experience provider, reaching new audiences on mobile phones at flexible subscription plans and low retail cost. We foster online discovery of new African voices and African literature for enthusiasts of all ages through our Playlists in English and local African languages.

One of the biggest barriers to literacy in Africa is simply access to books. Many children and young people do not have access to the books they need in their homes, schools and libraries. Audiobooks (and other forms of digital reading) provide another way to experience and enjoy books. I am creating a world where every young African can access the books they need to shape their lives – books that are in our own languages and relevant to our cultures.

AMABOOKS
ZIMBABWE

'amaBooks

PO Box AC 1066, Ascot, Bulawayo

amabooksbyo@gmail.com

amabooksbyo.blogspot.com

+44 1239 621841 : Jane Morris

amaBooks is a small, independent publisher based in
Zimbabwe's second city Bulawayo. We publish novels, short
stories, poetry, with a few local history and culture titles.
Our main focus is Zimbabwean literary fiction in English,
work that reflects contemporary life in the country. Since
our inception we have been able to give a platform to many
emerging writers, as well as those who are more established.
Over 200 writers have now been published by amaBooks.
Several of our titles have achieved recognition both nationally
and internationally, including those by Tendai Huchu,
Bryony Rheam, Togara Muzanenhamo, John Eppel,
Christopher Mlalazi and Pathisa Nyathi.

AMALION PUBLISHING
SENEGAL

📍 133 Cité Assembleé Ouakam BP 5637, Dakar-Fann, Dakar

@ publish@amalion.net

🌐 amalion.net

📞 +221 33 860 1904 : Sulaiman Adebowale

𝐟 AmalionPublishing　🐦 Amalion

Amalion Publishing is an independent scholarly publisher with
the mission to disseminate innovative knowledge on Africa
and to strengthen the understanding of Africa and its people.
Amalion provides a platform for authors to express new,
alternative and daring perspectives and views on people, places,
events, and issues shaping our world. Amalion Publishing
produces monographs, textbooks, journals and literary writing
– primarily in English and French – for scholars, students,
and general readers with an interest in African Studies, the
Humanities, and the Social Sciences. Amalion titles are
distributed in France and Benelux countries by l'Oiseau
Indigo and Bookwitty, in North America by International
Specialized Book Services and in the United Kingdom
by Central Books.

ATYPICAL BOOKS
FRANCE

⊙ 47 route des Pyrénées, Labatut-Rivière, 65700

@ ruth@ruthhartley.com

⊕ ruthhartley.com

🐦 ruthhartley9

👤 Ruth Hartley

I'm an independent writer who publishes Atypical Books about the untold stories, memoirs and resistance poems about those ordinary people often discounted by history. Atypical Books are for people trying to survive and make sense of extraordinary events in a rapidly changing global society that is moving from colonial to post-colonial cultures and economies. Atypical books are evocative, authentic and well-researched. They have complex rounded characters with realistic backstories representative of our multi-faceted world of diverse identities. The plots are well-structured page-turners. Environment and atmosphere are key while atypical historical fiction will also feel relevant and contemporary to its readers.

AYEBIA
UNITED KINGDOM

ayɛbia

7 Syringa Walk, Banbury, Oxfordshire, OX16 1FR

ayebia@ayebia.co.uk

ayebia.co.uk

+44 1295 709228 : Nana Ayebia Clarke MBE

Becky Nana Ayebia Clarke MBE is a Ghanaian-born award-winning Publisher. She was Submissions Editor at the African and Caribbean Writers Series at Heinemann Educational Books at Oxford where she worked for 12 years in the International Department that published and promoted award-winning writers to readers internationally. Writers published include Soyinka, Gordimer, Aidoo, Achebe, Ngugi, et al. She set up Ayebia with David her British husband in 2003 to look to new directions in African publishing after Heinemann stopped active publishing in the AWS in 2002.

Ayebia's mission is to open new spaces by offering fresh insights to this perspective. Ayebia books are used in faculties teaching African Studies as well as books for the ordinary reader about Africa and its Diasporas. Clarke was awarded an Honorary MBE in 2011 by Her Majesty Queen Elizabeth II for 'services to the UK publishing industry'.

AZTAR PRESS
SOUTH AFRICA

✉ P.O. Box 768, Morningside 2057, Gauteng

@ aztarpress@gmail.com

🌐 aztarpress.com

📞 +27 83 744 8277 : Judy Croome

f AztarPress   🐦 AztarPress   📷 aztar_press

In the time-honoured spirit of independent publishing,
Aztar Press is committed to publishing fiction and poetry
written outside the norms of the popular establishment.
The high-quality print and electronic books released by us
will share a common vision of fiction that both entertains
the reader and explores the authentic human experience.

BASLER AFRIKA BIBLIOGRAPHIEN
Namibia Resource Centre - Southern Africa Library

BASLER AFRIKA BIBLIOGRAPHIEN PUBLISHING HOUSE
SWITZERLAND

📍 Klosterberg 21, 4051 Basel, Switzerland

✉ Klosterberg 23, PO Box 4010, Basel, Switzerland

@ publishing@baslerafrika.ch   🌐 baslerafrika.ch/

📞 +41 61 228 93 33 : Petra Kerckhoff

f baslerafrika

The BAB Publishing House has been publishing scholarly works on Southern Africa, especially Namibia, since 1971. Its thematic emphases are oriented towards the humanities and social sciences. The BAB Publishing House seeks to promote cultural exchange and engagement regarding important contemporary historical issues and, in particular, to provide African scholars with a platform. Our (cultural-) historical, political and anthropological publications are aimed at international academic audiences as well as engaged readers broadly interested in Africa.

BHIYOZA PUBLISHERS (PTY) LTD
SOUTH AFRICA

⊙ 6443 Vermiculite Street, Johannesburg 1830

@ info@bhiyozapublishers.co.za

⊕ bhiyozapublishers.co.za

☎ +27 67 040 5029 : Menzi Thango

🐦 BhiyozaL   📷 Bhiyoza_Publishers

Bhiyoza Publishers is a small Black-owned company that specialises in publishing literary books written in African languages of South Africa. The founder and director of the company is Menzi Thango, an academic, editor, and author of isiZulu books. The company was established in 2018 and so far, it has published 35 books. We have mostly published in isiZulu, Sesotho and isiXhosa. Bhiyoza Publishers is committed to developing African languages and preserving the history, knowledge and ideas imbedded in these languages. We are interested in publishing creative works written by African writers, in an African context, about African people, their societal issues, lifestyles, politics, education and more.

BK PUBLISHING (PTY) LTD
SOUTH AFRICA

📍 1239 Francis Baard Street, Hatfield, Pretoria 0083

✉ P.O. Box 6314, Pretoria 0001

@ mail@bkpublishing.co.za

🌐 bkpublishing.co.za, supernovamagazine.co.za, preflightbooks.co.za

📞 +27 12 342 5347 : Benoit Knox

ⓕ supernovamag, PreflightBooks   ⓘ supernovamagazine, preflightbooks

BK Publishing is a vibrant publishing house in the heart of Pretoria. Our entrepreneurial spirit has manifested itself in the great variety of projects, imprints and services we provide. To fulfil our vision of fostering a book loving and book buying culture, we have created *Supernova*, the magazine for curious kids. With *Supernova* and other products for reluctant readers, we aim to make children aware of issues which affect them, their community and their environment. We give them the tools and inspiration to become active and responsible world citizens. With over 10 years of experience and a collection of wonderful original publications, our self-publishing division, Preflight Books, helps aspiring authors and self-publishers bring their manuscripts to life.

BLACKBIRD BOOKS
SOUTH AFRICA

593 Zone 4, Seshego, Polokwane 0742

23 Virgo, The Cosmos Estates, Kosmosdal, Centurion 0157

@ thabiso@blackbirdbooks.africa

blackbirdbooks.africa

+27 72 644 4771 : Thabiso Mahlape

BlackbirdBooks   _BlackBirdBooks   blackbirdbooks_africa

BlackBird Books was founded in August 2015 by publisher
Thabiso Mahlape. Its launch was a ground-breaking move
for the South African literary landscape and since its
inception we've been pioneering and establishing a home
for new African narratives, especially for Black authors.
Blackbird Books is concerned with publishing stories
that cut to the core and reflect the African experience.
We provide this platform to brilliant authors, concentrating
on young black authors, who would otherwise not have the
opportunity to tell the stories that shape and showcase the
wealth of their African experiences. We pride ourselves in
being a launchpad for black narratives that would otherwise
not get the attention they deserve.

BLUE WEAVER
SOUTH AFRICA

📍 Unit A, Victory Park, Lakeshore Road,
Capricorn Business Park, Muizenberg 7945

✉ PO Box 30370, Tokai, Cape Town 7966

@ info@blueweaver.co.za

🌐 blueweaver.co.za

📞 +27 21 701 4477

f blueweavermarketing 🐦 blueweaverpub 📷 blue_weaver

Established in 2000, Blue Weaver Marketing and Distribution
is today a leading independent distributor of local and
international specialist titles in South Africa. It provides a
direct marketing, sales and distribution infrastructure for
publishers and authors, allowing them to compete effectively
in the marketplace. The company promotes and sells to
academic institutions, bookshops, libraries, library suppliers
and specialist retailers throughout the SADC region.
Blue Weaver works in partnership with Booksite Afrika
who manages the physical distribution of its titles.
Blue Weaver also works closely with Books Direct, a
South African online retailer, and its subsidiary DigiThis,
a specialist ebook retailer.

BOOKCRAFT
NIGERIA

📍 23 Adebajo Street, Kongi Layout, Ibadan

✉ GPO Box 16729, Dugbe, Ibadan, Oyo State

@ info@bookcraftafrica.com

🌐 bookcraftafrica.com

📞 +234 8033447889,   +234 8073199967,
     +234 8037220773 : Yetunde Anifowoshe

f BookcraftAfrica   🐦 bookcraftafrica

Bookcraft Ltd is a publishing company. We have published
a large number of titles in a wide variety of subjects: art,
biography, history, literature, politics, and current affairs.
We publish for a growing market of discerning, sophisticated
and well-educated bibliophiles. Our books' uniquely
packaged, reader friendly design makes them instantly
recognisable.

BOOKSTORM
SOUTH AFRICA

BOOKSTORM

- 2nd Floor, Blackheath Mews, 258 Beyers Naude Drive, Blackheath 2195
- PO Box 4532, Northcliff, Johannesburg 2115
- info@bookstorm.co.za   bookstorm.co.za
- +27 11 478 6020
- Bookstorm   BookstormZA   bookstorm_za

Bookstorm is a boutique non-fiction book publishing company offering focused experience and innovation in the creation of books for the South African market. Bookstorm was founded in 2010 by Louise Grantham and Basil van Rooyen, both experienced trade publishers with a long history of publishing for the South African general reading market. We publish in a variety of genres including business, entrepreneurship, economics, investment, current affairs, cookery, health, sports and travel. Our books are written by a range of select South African authors who represent a diversity of skills and opinions. Bookstorm also offers agency distribution, corporate publishing services, and self-publishing services under its Rainbird imprint.

XMD BOOKS
BETTER IN THE SHORT RUN

34 CARLISE STREET, PAARDEN EILAND, CAPE TOWN 7405 SOUTH AFRICA

NEED TO PRINT BOOKS WITH QUANTITIES RANGING FROM 1 – Thousands?

Only print as and when you need.

We are based in Cape Town and service all publishers in
South Africa and Neighbouring Countries

Book Specifications we would need in order to send you a quotation:

Title   Quantity   Size   Text Colour & paper
Cover Board and Finish (ie; Gloss or MATT)
And Delivery address.

Do not hesitate to send your specifications to:

Glendor.crouch@xmdbooks.co.za ● Michael.White@xmdbooks.co.za ● Rieyaan.gamba@xmdbooks.co.za

Contacts:

Glendor +27105412110   Michael +27105412109   Rieyaan +27105412108

BOOK DASH
SOUTH AFRICA

@ team@bookdash.org

🌐 bookdash.org

👤 Julia Norrish

f bookdash   🐦 bookdash   📷 bookdash

At Book Dash, we believe every child should own a hundred books by the age of five. This means creating and distributing large numbers of new African storybooks in local languages. To make this possible, we gather creative professionals to create high-quality children's books that anyone can freely download, print, translate and distribute. We then work with funders and literacy and Early Childhood Development organisations to print and give away books in large volumes. Funders and partner organisations are encouraged to visit our website and get in contact with us.

BOOKS DIRECT
SOUTH AFRICA

Unit A, Victory Park, Lakeshore Road, Capricorn Business Park, Muizenberg 7945

PO Box 30370, Tokai, Cape Town 7966

admin@booksdirect.co.za   booksdirect.co.za/

+27 21 701 4477

booksdirectza   booksdirectza   booksdirectza

Books Direct is a new South African online book retailer that is run and managed by experienced, industry professionals. It focuses on selling a wide range of local and international Trade and Academic titles, in print format, at the most affordable prices. The ebook versions are sold through its subsidiary company, DigiThis. Books Direct focuses on giving customers a safe and secure, seamless and effortless experience in online shopping, from "Checking out" to "Delivered". The Company also effectively and proactively markets and promotes its Retail Platform, and the titles it has listed, to consumers and its customer base on a regular and ongoing basis.

BOOK LINGO
SOUTH AFRICA

📍 408 Elgin Avenue, Ferndale, Randburg 2194

@ publish@booklingo.co.za

🌐 booklingo.co.za

📞 +27 72 545 2366 : Clare-Rose Julius

ⓕ clarerose.julius   🐦 clarerose.julius

Book Lingo is a publishing start-up company. We work with many 'indie' authors, self-publishers and small independent publishing companies. The self-publishing landscape in South Africa has changed considerably over the past few years and it's a way for anyone to express their story in book form. We need to know and express our own stories in order to build a better South African society. We all have a story within us which needs to be told. Remember that your story may just change someone's life for the good. Be that change!

BREEZE PUBLISHING
SOUTH AFRICA

⊙ 15 Lavery Crescent, Overport, Durban 4091

@ breezepublishing@gmail.com

☎ +27 79 107 9930 : Naseema Mall

f breezepublishingcc

Breeze Publishing is set on publishing quality books of a variety of themes and categories, both in fiction and non-fiction; for the adult, teen and children's markets. Breeze Publishing is constantly being approached by both local and foreign authors, and continues to carefully select manuscripts of quality. The company has great aspirations to become a dominant player in a very versatile but restricted market and hopes to affiliate itself with both budding as well as established authors, so that it can grow with them to greater heights.

BRIGHT LIGHTS BOOKS
NIGERIA

Plot 2121 Ndola Crescent, Wuse Zone 5, Abuja,

contact@brightlightsbooks.com

brightlightsbooks.com

+234 906 617 4489 : Ese Emmanuel

brightlightsbooks   BrightLightsBks   bright_lights_books

We are a publisher of children's books by African writers aimed at a global African audience. Our goal is to educate and enlighten young readers through literature and art. We do this because we believe that through learning and education, children have a much better chance of achieving their goals and making an impact as adults. Also, we believe that the positive change we desire in our world begins with children.

BRIZA PUBLICATIONS
SOUTH AFRICA

BRIZA

⊙ 121 Southpansberg Road, Riviera, Pretoria 0084

@ christo@briza.co.za

⊕ briza.co.za

⊘ Christo Reitz

Briza Publications specialize in the publishing of botany and natural history books for the local and international market. All books are of high quality, have a practical approach and the content is informative. Briza was started in 1990 with the sole purpose of publishing an identification guide to grasses of South Africa. Now in its third edition, *Guide to Grasses of Southern Africa* is still a perennial bestseller! Our published list comprises of more than 130 products and includes definitive identification guides on medicinal plants, food plants, poisonous plants, indigenous plants, indigenous trees, indigenous garden plants, problem plants, wildflowers and plant groups such as aloes, succulents and orchids. Briza also publishes books on gardening, ecology, tourism, mammals, reptiles and birds.

BURNET MEDIA
SOUTH AFRICA

📍 PO Box 53557, Kenilworth, Cape Town 7745

@ info@burnetmedia.co.za

🌐 burnetmedia.co.za

👤 Tim Richman

f TwoDogsMercury   🐦 BurnetMedia

Burnet Media is an independent publisher based in Cape Town. We produce books for two main imprints – Two Dogs and Mercury, established in 2006 and 2011 respectively – as well as various customised publishing projects. As an authors' publisher our aim is to build close and interactive relationships with our authors and clients and, in doing so, create interesting and innovative titles for South Africa and the world. Jacana Media markets our titles into the trade.

Andy Thesen

DESKTOP PUBLISHING SERVICES
Full member Professional Editors' Guild

Experienced copy editor, book designer/typesetter
and proofreader, I work with fiction and poetry.
I produce ebooks and manage books through print.
Contact me at athesen@global.co.za or on +27 0827258801.

CATALYST PRESS
UNITED STATES

701 La Chapa Unit B, El Paso TX 79912

jlpowers@catalystpress.org

catalystpress.org

+1 925 315 5970 : Jessica Powers

catalystbooks2   catalyst_press   catalystpress

Change can be gradual, a slight shift that becomes a huge movement. Or it can be quick, a frenetic burst that suddenly makes everything new. But it all begins in the same way—with a spark, a catalyst. Catalyst Press was founded in 2017 as a literary spark. We publish books from and about Africa, stories that reveal the world from different perspectives and understandings. Publishing literary fiction, graphic novels, memoir, travel, crime fiction, and books for young readers, our authors explore lives, stories, and places in ways that make our global community feel more connected.

CHIMURENGA
SOUTH AFRICA

who no know go know

Room 303, Pan African Market, 76 Long Street, Cape Town

PO Box 15117, Vlaeberg, Cape Town 8018

@ chimurenga@panafrican.co.za, info@chimurenga.co.za

chimurenga.co.za

+27 21 422 4168

Chimurenga   Chimurenga_SA

Chimurenga is a journal of writing, art, culture and politics published out of Cape Town. Since its first issue (2002), *Chimurenga* has received excellent reviews for its originality, the quality of its content and its willingness to tackle subjects other publications might consider too difficult or controversial to address. Moreover, several contributors have won international awards for their work published in *Chimurenga*: Binyavanga Wainaina, Yvonne Adhiambo Owuor, Ishtiyaq Shukri, Chimamanda Ngozi Adichie and Seffi Atta to name a few.

CLOCKWORK BOOKS
SOUTH AFRICA

⊙ PO Box 44224, Linden 2104

@ info@worktheclock.co.za

⊕ ClockworkBooks.co.za

☎ +27 10 900 3164

(f) ClockworkBooksZA   🐦 clockwork_books   📷 clockwork_booksza

Independent publisher, publishing services provider and online bookstore based in Johannesburg, Clockwork Books' core mission is to support local authors by promoting outstanding South African books.

Our commitment to innovation enables us to reduce production costs without compromising on production standards, assuring our readers and clients of the best value for their money.

Our primary market is the South African family, and we develop our catalogue to meet their needs, delivering relevant, enjoyable, affordable fiction and nonfiction.

Our team of experienced publishing professionals deliver a full range of publishing services, from consulting and coaching, to editing, typesetting and project management.

COOKIEREADS
CANADA

📍 310 Cook Road, Toronto ON, M3J0C2

@ gozimbonu@yahoo.ca

🌐 cookiereads.com

📞 +1 64 7380 1119 : Ngozika Mbonu

f cookiereads   📷 cookiereads1

I write children's books because a child's formative life is very important. I want to ensure that children have the right attitude by writing stories that increase their confidence and self esteem.

DAVID PHILIP PUBLISHERS
TRADING AS NEW AFRICA BOOKS
SOUTH AFRICA

📍 Unit 13a, Athlone Industrial Park, 10 Mymoena Crescent, Athlone Industria 2, Cape Town 7764

✉ PostNet Suite144, Private Bag X9190, Cape Town 8000

@ info@newafricabooks.co.za

🌐 newafricabooks.co.za

📞 +27 21 467 5860 : Dusanka Stojakovic

ⓕ DavidPhilipPublishers   ⓨ _DavidPhilipPub   ⓞ newafricabooks

New Africa Books, incorporating David Philip Publishers, is one of South Africa's oldest and most prestigious independent publishing houses. With a history stretching back to the 1970s, our catalogue includes fiction and non-fiction titles for adults, YA and children. In recent years, we have moved our focus to publishing books for younger children in all eleven official languages. Recent award-winners are Lebohang Masango for *Mpumi's Magic Beads* (SALA; IBBY SA Picture Book Award; Pendoring Award), Nicolaas Maritz for (IBBY SA Picture book for his illustrations in *South African Animal Portraits – an A-Z* and a Pendoring Design Award for *Multilingual ABC*). Our content is fiercely African, and we are proud to have attracted many new voices to our stable – Loyiso Mkize (KWEZI comics); Buhle Ngaba; Nokuthula Mazibuko Msimang, and artists Nicolaas Maritz, Stanley Grootboom, Sam van Riet and Sanelisiwe Singaphi.

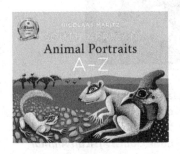

DEEP SOUTH
SOUTH AFRICA

deepsouth

📍 ISEA, Rhodes University, Makhanda 6140

@ info@deepsouth.co.za

🌐 africanbookscollective.com/publishers/deep-south

📞 +27 46 622 5081 : Robert Berold

Since 2000 deep south, run by Robert Berold, has been publishing bold and risk-taking South African writers, mostly poets. Authors include Seitlhamo Motsapi, Lesego Rampolokeng, Kelwyn Sole, Mxolisi Nyezwa, Angifi Dladla, Joan Metelerkamp, Vonani Bila, Khulile Nxumalo, Isabella Motadinyane, Alan Finlay, Mangaliso Buzani, Ayanda Billie, Haidee Kotze, Colleen Higgs and Chris van Wyk. Distribution of our books in South Africa is via Blue Weaver, who supply bookshops and libraries locally, and African Books Collective in the UK, who do international distribution and ebook publication. South African readers can also get books direct from deep south, pricelist available from us.

DIGITHIS
SOUTH AFRICA

- Unit A, Victory Park, Lakeshore Road, Capricorn Business Park, Muizenberg 7945
- PO Box 30370, Tokai, Cape Town 7966
- admin@booksdirect.co.za
- digithis.com/
- +27 21 701 4477

DigiThis is the ebook subsidiary of the online book retailer, Books Direct. Offering local and international ebook titles, DigiThis ensures a safe and secure shopping environment. It also offers customer support from industry professionals 24/7. With DigiThis, listed Publishers are secure in the knowledge that their content is protected by a well-recognised DRM service. Built on the industry standard Adobe Content Server, the same secure technology is used by giants such as Google, Barnes & Noble and Kobo. This allows for the simple process of Click, Download and Read and being able to provide ebooks anywhere on any device.

DRYAD PRESS
SOUTH AFRICA

⊙ 79 Brommersvlei Road, Constantia, Cape Town 7806

✉ Postnet Suite 281, Private Bag X16, Constantia, Cape Town 7484

@ business@dryadpress.co.za

⊕ dryadpress.co.za

☎ +27 83 408 3342 : Michèle Betty

ⓕ DryadPress 🐦 DryadPress 📷 DryadPresssa

Dryad Press is an independent publisher dedicated to
the promotion and publication of poetry in South Africa.
We publish poetry, which in the words of Roland Barthes,
searches for "the inalienable meaning of things".
Our determinant for publication, is the ability of the
literature to defamiliarise. Innovative and exciting poetry
that surprises, not only in form and technique, but also in its
ability to enable us to reflect on our experiences in the world
in a new way. Dryad Press aims to unlock South African
voices that present their stories in a fresh light and, in so
doing, to nurture a new generation of South African poets.

ÉDITIONS GRAINES DE PENSÉES
TOGO

30 Boulevard du 13 Janvier, Nyékonakpoè – Lomé 07 B.P. 7097

grainesdepensees@yahoo.com

afrilivres.net

+228 90 32 33 20, +228 22 22 32 43 : Mrs Yasmin Issaka-Coubageat

editions.grainesdepensees

At Graines de Pensées we want to participate in African cultural expression, to contribute, with our books, to the development of a democratic and pluralist society, with the ability to criticize and respond to social issues. As publishers we are keen to give to this new African generation books that are accessible, that they can relate to, and that have a very high editorial quality. Furthermore, for a better distribution of our books, we participate in co-publishing projects, with partners in countries in both the South and the North. We also create business relationships with various institutions and companies for the better promotion of books in French, English and African languages.

EDITORA TRINTA ZERO NOVE
MOZAMBIQUE

⊙ 1042, Amílcar Cabral Ave, Maputo 1100

✉ PO Box 3672, Maputo 1100

@ contacto@editoratrintazeronove.org

⊕ editoratrintazeronove.org

☎ +258 847 003 009 : Sandra Tamele

f editoratrintazeronove 🐦 TrintaZero 📷 editoratrintazeronove

Editora Trinta Zero Nove is an independent press based in
Maputo, Mozambique. It was started in 2018 by Sandra
Tamele to publish the collection of short fiction translated
by the winners of the literary translation competition that
celebrates International Translation Day, 30 September.
This initiative was awarded a Special Mention on the London
Book Fair Excellence Awards in 2020. Editora Trinta Zero
Nove wants to be inclusive by translating and publishing
mostly female writers and writers with disabilities or from
other minorities in both print and audiobook formats.
Its catalogue is known for featuring many debuts in
translation into Mozambican languages.

EN TOUTES LETTRES
MOROCCO

⊙ 28 avenue des F.A.R, app. 59 - 20000, Casablanca

@ info@etlettres.com

⊕ etlettres.com

☎ +212 5 22 29 68 48 : Kenza Sefrioui

f etlettres 🐦 etlettres 📷 etlettres

EN TOUTES LETTRES is an independent publishing company based in Casablanca, specialized in essays by writers, researchers and journalists, in order to spread culture of debate and critical thinking. Since 2014, we published 16 titles, in French and Arabic, in 5 series, like *Enquêtes* (*Investigation*) and *Les Questions qui fâchent* (*The Troublesome Issues*). Our books won the Grand Atlas Prize three times, and some titles reach more than 3 500 copies sold, and were translated into Spanish and Italian. EN TOUTES LETTRES is a member of the International Alliance of Independent Publishers, and also runs Openchabab.com, a training program for young journalists, which teachs both the methods of independent journalism and humanist values, and helps them become authors.

FEMRITE – UGANDA WOMEN WRITERS ASSOCIATION
UGANDA

⊙ Kira Road Plot 147, Kampala 705

@ info@femriteug.org

⊕ femriteug.org

☎ +256 414 543 943 : Hilda Twongyeirwe

ⓕ FemriteUg   ⓨ ugwomenwriters

FEMRITE publishes fiction and creative non-fiction which is mainly written by women. From establishment, the organizsation was aimed at training, promoting and publishing women writers. This still has a big bearing on what is published because women's situations which led to the establishing of the organisation have not changed substantially. However, FEMRITE has included male writers in its programmes because both male and female writers operate under the same infrastructure and some issues such as limited publishing opportunities affect them in the same way.

FUNDZA LITERACY TRUST
SOUTH AFRICA

fun·D·za

⊙ Suite B2A, Westlake Square, 1 Westlake Drive, Westlake 7950

@ info@fundza.co.za

⊕ fundza.co.za/

☎ +27 21 709 0688 : Mignon Hardie & Zilungile Zimela

ⓕ FunDzaLiteracyTrust ⓦ FunDzaClub

The FunDza Literacy Trust believes that reading changes lives. Its mission is to get young South Africans – specifically those from poor backgrounds with little access to books – reading and writing for pleasure. Through FunDza's 'cellphone library' - fundza.mobi - it is creating, commissioning, curating and publishing new local stories, books, blogs and articles to inspire a lifelong love of reading and stories. More than 200,000 unique users connect with FunDza's network every month.

FunDza's innovative approach to developing readers and writers has received local and international recognition. In 2017, it was awarded the inaugural Joy of Reading Award, a Gold Impumelelo Social Innovation Award, and the UNESCO Confucius Prize for Literacy.

More from Lebohang Masango

AVAILABLE IN ALL ELEVEN OFFICIAL SOUTH AFRICAN LANGUAGES

Winner of 3 awards:
IBBY Writers Award, The 2019 S.A Literary Award, The GOLD Pendoring Award

The beads jingle, jangle and sparkle. The girls giggle with glee! Mpumi and her friends discover magic in her hair and what begins as an ordinary school day in Joburg is suddenly full of adventure everywhere!
Mpumi's Magic Beads is a delightful story about friendship, self-esteem, discovery and beautiful hair in the big city of Joburg.

NEW FROM NOKUTHULA MAZIBUKO MSIMANG

Who is Caster Semenya? Where did she grow up?

Caster Semenya is the FASTEST girl on earth!

Follow Caster's journey to become the fastest girl on earth. Beautifully illustrated by Sanelisiwe Singaphi.

This story will be available in all 11 South African languages

New Africa Books
orders@newafricabooks.co.za
021 467 5860
Unit 13, Athlone Industrial Park, 10 Mymoena Crescent, Cape Town

HANDS-ON BOOKS
SOUTH AFRICA

⊙ 50 Geluks Road, Sybrand Park 7700

@ info@modjajibooks.co.za : Colleen Higgs

(f) handsonbooksza

An imprint of Modjaji Books. We make beautiful books and assist you with editing, design, proofreading, printing PR – all the things you need to successfully publish your book. We can also offer distribution into the South African and international markets. We also offer other services such as manuscript assessment and individual consultations about publishing, as well as seminars on publishing options and how to publish successfully in South Africa.

HUZA PRESS
RWANDA

⊙ Street KN 14, House No. 21, Kigali

✉ PO Box 1610, Kigali

@ huzapress@gmail.com

⊕ huzapress.com

☏ +250 784575762 : Lucky Grace Isingizwe

🅕 Huzapress   🅦 huzapress   🅞 huzapress

Huza Press is a Rwanda based publishing house that
publishes Rwandan, East African, and African writers based
on the continent or outside. We accept work in English,
French, or Kinyarwanda, and we publish fiction (novels
and collections of short stories), creative nonfiction, and
collections of poetry. We are committed to developing
quality creative writing, celebrating and publishing literary
works from the continent through workshops, literary
events, and book publishing projects.

IMPEPHO PRESS
SOUTH AFRICA

PO Box 12258, Queenswood, Pretoria 0121

getinfo@impephopress.co.za

impephopress.co.za

+27 82 330 7249 : Sarah Godsell

impephop   impephop

impepho press is a Pan Africanist publishing house committed to the sincere telling of African and international stories, celebrating both the fragility and resilience of the human experience. We believe in championing brave, particularly feminist, voices committed to literary excellence.

We pride ourselves on providing our authors with the best editorial, design and promotional support as possible, irrespective of the stages in their careers. At impepho press, we serve the stories, always! Because without our stories, we would, in the words of Audre Lorde, be crumpled into other people's fantasies of us and eaten alive.

IWALEWABOOKS
NIGERIA, GERMANY, SOUTH AFRICA

⊙ Paradise Jetty, Plot 8, Walter Carrington Crescent,
   Victoria Island, Lagos

@ info@iwalewabooks.com

⊕ iwalewabooks.com

ⓕ iwalewabooks   ⓞ iwalewabooks

iwalewabooks is a publishing house for art and discourse.
Through a number of series, we dedicate our publications
to questions about aesthetic social discourses, the politics
of collecting and debates about archives and artistic and
academic positions from the Global South. All publications
are based on the conviction that creating books is an
aesthetic and collective endeavour. Many volumes are
therefore produced in collaboration with research projects
as well as cultural and societal initiatives.

We are currently based in Bayreuth (Germany),
Johannesburg (South Africa) and Lagos (Nigeria).

JACANA MEDIA
SOUTH AFRICA

JACANA MEDIA
We publish what we like

10 Orange Street, Sunnyside, Auckland Park, Johannesburg 2092

PO Box 291784, Melville, Johannesburg 2109

marketing@jacana.co.za

jacana.co.za

+27 011 628 3200 : Bridget Impey and Maggie Davey

Jacana Media   jacanamedia   jacanamedia

We are a ground-breaking and fiercely independent publisher, producing books in the fields of the arts, natural history, lifestyle, fiction, South African history, current affairs, memoir and biography, children's books and public health. We publish work from some of the most imaginative, award-winning and clear-thinking minds of our time. Our books respond to the challenges of the moment and certainly inform and frequently change the national conversation.

Jacana Media won the Bologna Book Fair award for Best African Children's Publisher in 2018. We have made it a proud tradition to publish in all 11 official South African languages.

JUNKETS PUBLISHER
SOUTH AFRICA

Junkets Publisher

✉ PO Box 38040, Pinelands, Cape Town 7430

@ info.junkets@iafrica.com

🌐 junkets.co.za

📞 +27 78 763 3177, +27 76 169 2789 : Andi Mgibantaka & Robin Malan

ⓕ groups/Junkets, Junketspublisher, Junkets10Series

Junkets Publisher is a small not-for-profit independent publisher that specialises in high-quality low-cost new South African playscripts. We publish the Playscript Series of individual plays, the Collected Series of anthologies of plays, and the Junkets10Series of ten new plays celebrating our tenth birthday in 2015. The BaxterJunkets series publishes the winning play of each year's Zabalaza Theatre Festival. GayJunkets publishes queer-interest books in various genres. The first book we published in 2005 was *Rebel Angel*, a novel based on the life of John Keats. 'Junkets' is Leigh Hunt's nickname for him: Jun-Kets. Our logo is Keats's autograph.

KACHIFO
NIGERIA

Prestige

📍 253 Herbert Macaulay Way, Yaba, Lagos

@ info@kachifo.com

🌐 kachifo.com, farafinabooks.wordpress.com

📞 +234 8077364217

👍 farafinabook 🐦 farafinabooks

Kachifo Limited, an independent Nigerian publishing house, began operations in 2004 driven by the words of its motto and mission statement, Telling our own Stories. Its imprint, Farafina, has published works of fiction, memoirs, and poetry with an African audience in mind. It continues to receive unsolicited submissions at submissions@kachifo.com

KHALOZA BOOKS
SOUTH AFRICA

📍 6 Frolich Street, Parys, Free State

✉ PO Box 998, Parys, Free State 9585

@ info@khalozabooks.com

🌐 khalozabooks.com

👤 Thato Motaung

📘 KhalozaBooks   🐦 KhalozaBooks   📷 KhalozaBooks

Khaloza Books was established in 2017, as a Pan-African publishing house for books – fiction and non-fiction – about Africa for children and young adults. We are passionate about capturing, and promoting African stories in our indigenous languages, because we believe that as Africans we need to take ownership of our own narratives, and enforce a culture of reading and writing. Join us as we #ReadWriteAfrican

LOGOS OPEN CULTURE
MALAWI

⊙ The Culture Lab, Four Seasons Centre, Presidential Way, Lilongwe

✉ P.O Box 30906, Lilongwe

@ logosopenculture@gmail.com, muti@logosmw.org

⊕ logosmw.org

☎ +265 99 63 76 788 : Mutisunge Michael Etter-Phoya

ⓕ lovesMalawi   🐦 logosMLW

Our customers are interested in participating in Malawi's
story. They are on the look-out for new, accessible and
carefully-crafted books about Malawi. We create well-
researched content that celebrates Malawi's rich diversity.

MARKETFIFTYFOUR.COM
ONLINE

@ info@marketfiftyfour.com, Marthe@marketfiftyfour.com

⊕ MarketFiftyFour.com

⊗ Marthe van der Wolf

(f) marketfiftyfour   ⊚ marketfiftyfour   ⊚ marketfiftyfour

MarketFiftyFour.com is an online bookshop for mostly
African language books by African authors, on the
continent and in the diaspora. MarketFiftyFour.com
publishes affordable ebooks, Audiobooks, and paperbacks.
Current publications include books, short stories, and
poetry in Somali, Amharic, Ga, Tigrinya, Kinyarwanda,
Kiswahili, Twi, and English.

MODJAJI BOOKS
SOUTH AFRICA

50 Geluks Road, Sybrand Park 7700

info@modjajibooks.co.za

modjajibooks.co.za

+27 72 774 3546 : Colleen Higgs

Modjajibooks   modjaji_bks   modjajibooks

Modjaji Books is an independent publishing company based in Cape Town and is a member of the International Alliance of Independent Publishers. We publish books by southern African women writers – novels, short stories, memoir, biography, poetry, essays, narrative non-fiction by women writers.

The history of publishing in South Africa is enmeshed with the culture of resistance that flourished under apartheid.

We continue to promote local women's voices, and are pleased to note that this focus has now been taken up by most trade publishers in South Africa. Modjaji titles are true to the spirit of Modjaji, the rain queen: a powerful female force for good, growth, new life, regeneration.

Our books are distributed locally by Protea Boekehuis into the trade. African Books Collective distributes our titles internationally.

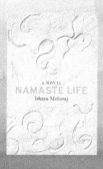

Tortoise and Ostrich
By Katrina Esau

A delightful folk tale from the
Northern Karoo, and the very first
children's book to feature a story
for children, in the N|uu language.
There are only five N|uu speakers
in the world. This tale about
Tortoise and Ostrich is written in
N|uu, Afrikaans and English.

The very first children's book in the Nluu language

!Qhoi n|a Tjhoi
Skilpad en Volstruis
Tortoise and Ostrich

Story by Katrina Esau, as told to Claudia Snyman
Illustrations by Stanley Grootboom

New Africa Books

021 467 5860   orders@newafricabooks.co.za

PALACE OF KNOWLEDGE (PTY) LTD
SOUTH AFRICA

PALACE OF KNOWLEDGE

📍 320 Dr Pixley Kaseme Street, Durban 4001

✉ P.O BOX 4948, QUALBERT 4078

@ info@palacek.co.za

🌐 palacek.co.za

📞 +27 67 888 4323 : Qiniso Ncwane

Palace of Knowledge is a private company specialising in book publishing. It is a member of the Durban Chamber Of Commerce (DCC). It is also registered under the Central Suppliers Database (CSD). Palace of Knowledge is a Broad Based Black Economic Empowerment (BBBEE) compliant Company.

We publish the following: Awareness and motivational books, educational books, fiction and non-fiction, religion, historical, cultural, children's books, learners' magazines, learners' newspaper, educational games and educational charts. The company also offers the following services: editing, proof reading, book cover design, illustrations, author's marketing material (website, banners, caps, T-shirts), printing (books, newsletters, magazines, booklets).

PARRÉSIA PUBLISHERS LTD
NIGERIA

📍 82 Allen Avenue, Ikeja, Lagos

@ info@parresia.com.ng

🌐 parresia.com.ng

📞 +234 815 458 2178 : Azafi Omoluabi-Ogosi

f ParresiaPublishers   🐦 Parresiabooks   📷 Parresiapublishers

We are a publishing company based in Lagos, Nigeria.
We comprise teams of diverse professionals banded together
for one purpose—producing great books, your books!
This synergy informs our company motto—Your words …
in Trust!

PELMO BOOK PUBLISHERS
SOUTH AFRICA

📍 202 Gary Avenue, Waterkloof Glen, Pretoria 0181

✉ PO Box 10922, Centurion 0046

@ info@pelmobooks.co.za

🌐 pelmopublishers.co.za

📞 +27 12 771 7713 : Nkemiseng Molefe

𝑓 Pelmo Publishers   🐦 pelmopublishers   📷 pelmopublishers

Pelmo Book Publishers was officially established in 2012 by director, Nkemiseng Molefe, at the age of 25 years. Our mission as a literature hub is to make sure that our nation's indigenous languages are not only passed on generation-to-generation through speech, but that our people are also educated in and about their home languages. By publishing books in South African languages, we encourage people to learn, read, write and speak in their mother tongues and even more, to write books in their own languages.

POETREE PUBLICATIONS
SOUTH AFRICA

⊙ 217 Textile House, 125 Kerk Street, Johannesburg 2000

@ poetflow@live.com

☏ +27 73 652 0275 : Selome Payne (Flow)

𝐟 poetreepub   🐦 PoetreeBooks

Poetree Publications strives to provide affordable and accessible publishing services to writers of all genres, and change the perceptions of self-publishing as a whole. Our mission is to make a significant contribution to the publication of new work by African writers, especially African literature titles. Poetree aims to immortalise and preserve the stories and indigenous languages of writers, especially the youth, by offering self-publishing services for poetry, fiction/non-fiction, children's stories, motivational books, short stories and more. Services include publishing in print and e-formats.

PROFOUNDER PUBLISHERS
SOUTH AFRICA

INTELLIGENCE | MANAGEMENT | SERVICES

📍 181 Corlett Drive, Bramley, Johannesburg 2090

✉ 92176, Norwood, Johannesburg 2117

@ info@profounder.co.za

🌐 profounder.co.za

📞 +27 114407501 : Victorine Mbong Shu

ⓕ profounderintelligence 🐦 ProfounderSA

Profounder Publishing and Self-Publishing is a division
of Profounder Intelligence Management Services CC which
has been in business of education and training since 2007.
Following popular demand, a publishing division was
established in 2015. Since then, we publish books and
facilitated the release of music, movies and theatre. We pride
ourselves on our speed and efficiency in producing award-
winning authors. We can work with you from the beginning
of the process, or after you send us your manuscript.
We own an exciting video and audio studio equipped
and ready for you. We can also market your work.

PROTEA BOEKHUIS /
PROTEA BOOK HOUSE
SOUTH AFRICA

PROTEA

⊙ 8 Minni Street, Clydesdale, Pretoria

✉ P O Box 35110, Menlo Park 0102

@ info@proteaboekhuis.co.za

🌐 proteaboekhuis.com

☎ +27 12 343 6279

Ⓕ Protea Boekhuis   Ⓘ proteaboekhuis

Currently, Protea Boekhuis specialises, among other things, in the publication of Afrikaans poetry and plays, translations into Afrikaans of the best children's titles available all over the world, leading non-fiction, and South African history.

REAMSWORTH PUBLISHING
NIGERIA

No. 15, Road A, Unique Estate, Off Powerline, Ibadan-Oyo Express Way, Ibadan

U.I. P.O. Box 23182, U.I. Post Office, Ibadan

@ reamswortheducation@gmail.com

reamsworthpublishing.com

+234 8038571870

Reamsworth Learning   Reamsworth1   reamsworth

Reamsworth Publishing is poised to produce scholarly, academic and educational books in Africa. It is founded by a scholarly passion to promote and communicate knowledge from Africa. Its founding is based on the principle that to promote knowledge and present the true African realities it is better done by Africans and this ultimately matters in development.

KWEZI
EDITION 5, ISSUES 13 TO 15

**One of the first comics in SA to portray South African Superheros
by Loyiso Mkize**

There is chaos in Gold City! An unexpected twist to the prophecy has given rise to the original star child, Nerus: but why does the great Aarik himself, Nerus and his sprawling army descend on the city, destroying everything in its wake?

ISBN: 978-1-4856-3023-4
Language: English
Available at New Africa Books
www.newafricabooks.com
021 467 5860

MORE OF KWEZI COMICS

Collectors Edition 1 includes the first three issues of the KWEZI comics. Created by South African artist Loyiso Mkize, KWEZI is the classic young hero in a coming of age tale.

ISBN: **978 1 4856 2272 7** (English)
Language: English, French, IsiXhosa, IsiZulu, Sesotho

The African superhero is back! In Collectors Edition 2, KWEZI hones his superhuman abilities and accepts that his powers are to be used to save his homeland from evil forces.

ISBN: **978 1 4856 2297 0** (English)
Language: English, French, IsiXhosa, IsiZulu

Power hungry Mr. Mpisi and his cohorts plot to stop the rise of KWEZI and the superhero trio.

ISBN: **978 1 4856 2581 0** (English
Language: English, IsiZulu

Mr. Mpisi tries to create an anti-superhero campaign which culminates in a showdown in the desert. Is the story fact or a lie?

ISBN: **978-1-4856-2705-0** (English)
Language: English

Available at New Africa Books
www.newafricabooks.com
021 467 5860

SAMNKO BOOKS
SOUTH AFRICA

⊙ Office 0813, 14 Bureau Lane, Rentbel Tower,
Pretoria Central, 0002

@ Info@samnko.co.za

⊕ samnko.co.za

☏ +27 12 023 2182 : Sam Nkogatse

ⓕ Samnko Books   🐦 SamnkoBooks   📷 SamnkoBooks

We focus on assisting emerging writers who wish to see their
words in print and to retain control of their rights, our aim
is to contribute to the development of African language
through literature, adding value to the importance of
reading. We offer the following services: ghost writing,
assisted self-publishing, book design, marketing and
distribution, printing and capacity building.

SEDIA
ALGERIA

📍 Cité les mandariniers, Lot 293, Al Mohammadia 16211, Alger

@ BP 231, Al Mohammadia

🌐 sedia@sedia-dz.com

📞 +213 770 973 861 : Nacéra Khiat

ⓕ sediaalgiers

SEDIA is an Algerian publishing house created in March, 2000 known for editing curricular and extra-curricular books before becoming in 2006 a non-specialized publishing house with the peculiarity to republish famous Algerian novelists from abroad as their several translated work, such as Mohammed Dib and Assia Djebar.

With its rich and varied catalogue, between novels, essays, beautiful books and comic books besides preschool methods and extracurricular books, SEDIA detains a considerable place in the field of the Algerian books today not only as publisher but also as importer of books.

SEFSAFA CULTURE & PUBLISHING
EGYPT

4 Soliman Gohar Sq. Dokki, Giza

elbaaly@gmail.com, info@sefsafa.net

sefsafa.net

+20 1110787870, +20 1275324306 : Mohamed El-Baaly

sefsafa   Sefsafapub

Sefsafa Culture & Publishing is a small group based in
Egypt, working under the umbrella of 'Sefsafa Culture &
Publishing'. We have had a publishing house since 2009, and
have published over 100 titles, one third of them translations.
The group has also organized the Cairo Literature Festival
since 2015, and the Egypt Comix Week festival since 2014.
Sefsafa aims to support the enlightenment and Arab
Spring ideals.

SHAMA
ETHIOPIA

⊙ PO Box 57, Piazza in front of Cathedral School, Addis Ababa

@ shama@ethionet.et, gbagersh@shamaethipia.com

⊕ shamaethiopia.com

☏ +251 115545290 : Ghassan Bagersh

Shama Books, fully owned by the Bagersh family, has been involved in the publishing of books since 1999, making it the premier mass market publisher in Ethiopia. Shama boasts a burgeoning publishing house that attracts the finest Ethiopian writers, as well as many established foreign authors. Shama, with a mission of improving literacy at all levels and fostering a reading culture in the country, has published over a hundred titles. In addition to operating a chain of BookWorld bookshops we also operate newsstands and souvenir shops in the major five star hotels in Addis Ababa.

STORY PRESS AFRICA
SOUTH AFRICA

P.O. Box 22106, Mayor's Walk 3208

@ info@storypressafrica.com

storypressafrica.com

+27 76 173 7130 : Robert Inglis

storypressafrica   catalyst_press   catalystpress

Story Press Africa is a celebration of African knowledge. Humankind emerged in Africa, and with humans came stories as a means for sharing knowledge between people, through the generations. The rich and vibrant storytelling tradition of Africa is reflected in the visually exciting and compelling narratives of Story Press Africa's books, linking us all to our earliest roots and to one another. Discover the stories which are part of all of our stories. Story Press Africa: African knowledge. African Stories. Worldwide.

Story Press Africa is distributed in the US by Consortium and in Southern Africa by Lapa Uitgewers - lapa@lapa.co.za

THEART PRESS
SOUTH AFRICA

⊙ 229 The Quays, Park Lane, Century City, Cape Town

✉ Suite 271, Private Bag X1005, Claremont, Cape Town 7735

@ theartpressbooks@gmail.com

🌐 theartpressbooks.com/

📞 +27 61 508 4691 : Taryn Lock

🅕 theartpressbooks 🐦 Theart_Press 📷 theart_press

Theart Press is a South African publisher that specialises in inspirational poetry, children's books and autobiographies. We hope to help Africans to share their stories. Profits go to literacy non-profit organisation Read to Rise.

UNIVERSITY OF NAMIBIA PRESS
NAMIBIA

📍 340 Mandume Ndemufayo Ave, Pionierspark, Windhoek

✉ Private Bag 13301, Windhoek

@ unampress@unam.na

🌐 unam.edu.na/unam-press

📞 +264 61 206 4714 : Dr Jill Kinahan

UNAM Press publishes works on topics related to Namibia and the Southern African region. Published and forthcoming titles include studies of literature, language and culture; education and democracy; statutory and customary law; public policy; social and political history; autobiographies; and indigenous knowledge.

WEAVER PRESS
ZIMBABWE

⊙ 38 Broadlands Road, Emerald Hill, Harare

✉ P.O. Box A1922, Avondale, Harare

@ weaveradmin@mango.zw

⊕ weaverpresszimbabwe.com

☎ +263 4 308330 : Njabulo Mbono

Weaver Press is a small publishing house committed to the production and distribution of the best of Zimbabwe's creative writing and scholarly research. It was established in 1998, since when it has developed a solid reputation for excellent editorial and production standards. As well as publishing contemporary fiction, we work with researchers and academic authors to produce books which reflect the developing tensions, challenges and prospects for Zimbabwean society; we also, on occasion, undertake freelance editing and typesetting.

YIZ HOUSE PUBLISHING
SOUTH AFRICA

YIZ
PUBLISHING

📍 84 Impala Crescent, Extension 5, Lenasia 1820
✉ P.O.Box 700, Lenasia 1820
@ YizHousePublishing@gmail.com
📞 +27 82 629 8663 : Dr Zaheera Jina
🅕 Yiz House Publishing   📷 yizhousepublishing

Yiz House Publishing is a boutique book publishing company presenting dedicated involvement and creation in the conception of books for the South African market. The company was started by Dr Zaheera Jina Asvat. We publish books for children ages 8 to 16, written by children ages 8 to 16. Our focus is currently on fiction anthologies for younger readers.

We offer tailored online writing mentorships that address figurative language to teach children between the ages of 8 and 16, to dress their words. Our writers create poetry, descriptions and short stories of 2000 words. We publish the collections. Our books include: *Tween Tales: The Adventure Begins; Tween Tales 2: Adventure Camp* and *Almost Me.*

ZAZI BOOKS
SOUTH AFRICA

✉ PO Box 44224, Linden, Johannesburg 2104

@ hello@zazibooks.co.za

🌐 ZaziBooks.co.za

📞 +27 010 900 3164

Books kids want to read. Driven by our conviction in the wide-ranging benefits of reading for pleasure, Zazi Books publishes the best local fiction for tweens (8 to 12 years old) in English, isiZulu and isiXhosa. We seek out the newest, quirkiest, most exciting South African voices in middle grade fiction to thrill and enchant our audience, and we are committed to producing books that are affordable and relevant. Zazi Books, kubomnandi!

CLASSIFIEDS

MARGOT BERTELSMANN
Copy editing, proofreading and beta reading of fiction and nonfiction manuscripts. / mb4774@gmail.com

TAMARA GUHRS
Tamara Guhrs is a freelance writer, researcher, editor and proof reader specialising in pictorial books, academic theses, education textbooks, dramatic arts, development and culture. Tamara has experience managing small print or online publication projects, from concept development and writing to design and production. She has a creative, problem-solving outlook, a stringent eye for detail, and is uncompromising on quality.
tamara@notacontentwriter.com / www.notacontentwriter.com
+27 073 2270777

MARIANNE VALENTINE
I proofread Afrikaans to a high standard (where I adhere closely to the Afrikaanse Woordelys en Spelreëls) and English. I can translate your copy accurately from Afrikaans to English and vice versa.
marianne1971valentine0520@gmail.com / +27 082 3705580

CATHY DIPPNALL
Specialising in academic and business editing, non-fiction editing including religion and biographies, ghostwriting, research and proofreading services.
cathyd.eish@gmail.com / www.eishcomm.com / +27 084 2403516

ARTICLES

Publishing in the pandemic: Africa in Words interviews publishers about how they are surviving these times

by Aimee-Claire Smith

In the early days of the pandemic, Africa in Words started Words on the Times – a Q&A series inspired by the spirit of community and resilience, initiated to connect the blog's communities of work and life through their experiences of the COVID-19 pandemic.

As Goretti Kyomuhendo, chair of the AKO Caine Prize, put it in her piece for Words of the Times, "Covid profoundly changed or affected the everyday working lives of everyone." We all know all too well that bookmaking has never been an easy or simple task, and the pandemic throws yet another spanner – or several – in the works.

Words on the Times allows a space for African publishers, writers, and others involved in the bookmaking ecosystem to commiserate, share what they have found uplifting, and put out calls for support. To date, Words on the Times has published interviews with Lizzy Attree of Short Story Day Africa, Nzube Nlebedim of The Shallow Tales Review, Zimbabwean writer Tinashe Mushakavanhu, and others. The full archive of conversations can be found on the Africa in Words website.

Many have found the endearing quality of books and literature to be heartening, an anchor in unsteady seas. Ellenore Angelidis, of Open Hearts Big Dreams & Ready Set Go Books, shares that "Seeing those books getting loved and appreciated around the world by those who enjoy the stories, as well as

 THIS PAGE WAS GENEROUSLY SPONSORED BY FIONA ROSS

the art of our friend who lives in my daughter's birthplace, is a gift that continues to give joy and hope." Meron Hadero, whose short story "The Street Sweep" was shortlisted for the 2021 AKO Cane Prize, says that "The consistency of writing for me has been a wonderful steadying force in an unpredictable time."

Others have found an unexpected lighthouse of hope and possibility in the COVID-induced shift to living our lives largely online. M Lynx Qualey of ArabLit says: "On the positive side, space has opened up for a lot more digital events. Along with Sawad Hussain, we're helping organize BILA HUDOOD: Arabic Literature Everywhere, a three-day literary festival coming in July. We'd never have been able to get the funds for an in-person literary festival, but a relatively modest 3500 pound grant will be enough to help us get a digital festival off the ground."

The series also features interviews with those who often work behind the scenes and more broadly, such as editors, those who produce literary magazines, and publicists. Dami Ajayi, one of the editor's of Limbe to Lagos, shares that "Lockdowns have meant that we invent new ways of working, relying heavily on technology. As a writer, however, the work has hardly changed, because it is still that solitary experience of staring at a blank page and blinking cursor."

Meanwhile, Francis Nyamnjoh and Kathryn Toure from

THIS PAGE WAS GENEROUSLY SPONSORED BY FIONA ROSS

Langaa RPCIG remind us that "what the crisis seems to suggest is the importance of bringing the virtual and the face-to-face into greater conversation in telling African stories and in researching, publishing, and sharing the continent's experiences. This is an opportune time to explore and open up intersecting identities and relations, question stereotypes and biases, and counter systemic suppression and oppression."

Goretti Kyomuhendo, who is also director of the African Writers Trust, has found that the pandemic allowed them "to plan for the future. Having cancelled or postponed all our activities last year, and many this year, we used the time and resources to establish a writers' training centre, a pioneering initiative intended to fill a literary gap in the East and the Horn of Africa sub-region."

As important as it is to hold onto hope, sometimes things also just aren't sunshine and rainbows. Sometimes all you can do, in the words of Modjaji Books' Colleen Higgs, is "keep things ticking over".

Nick Mulgrew of uHlanga shares, "There hasn't been a great amount of levelheaded, public honesty about how difficult this has been: we're always looking for the positive angle, or the deft and lucid summation of the medical-political omnishambles we've been living through. I think it's enough to say that it's been horrible, it is continuing to be horrible, and that I cannot wait for it to be over. People have been and haven't been supportive; what lifts the heart one day doesn't work the next."

And looking ahead? While none of us can accurately predict what the world – and the literary landscape – will look like once the storm of COVID has fully passed and the dust settled, Poda-Poda Stories's Ngozi Cole is "really excited for the art and cultural scenes beyond COVID. I think staying indoors has given a lot of creatives time to reflect and refocus, as well as get creative ideas on how we can harness technology and the digital world for creativity. That really uplifts me, that no matter what's going on in the world, art and creativity can still shine through."

courses for people passionate about writing

Do you dream of publishing your book?

But you need help to get it to a publishable standard?

Or you need help with transforming your idea into a compelling story?

We can help.

Our **Creative Writing Course** will equip you with the range of skills you need to write – or rewrite – your book.

Our **Literary Assessment** will identify your writing's strengths – and its weaknesses.

Our **Mentoring Programme** will, month-by-month, drive you through the process of actually writing your book.

Our **Book Doctor** will work with you to tauten your story, develop your characters and enrich your voice.

Contact us to discuss your needs.

We can help.

admin@allaboutwritingcourses.com
www.allaboutwritingcourses.com

What is Book Dash?

by Julia Norrish

Book Dash is a South African social impact publisher of free books for very young children. Our vision is that "Every child should own a hundred books by the age of five", before they enter school!

To that end, Book Dash gathers creative professionals who volunteer to create new, African storybooks that anyone can freely translate and distribute. We employ our unique, 12-hour book-making methodology to create beautiful new books in just one day! Everything we make on that day is a gift to the world. That means we share the books freely on our website (bookdash.org) and in physical format for children to own.

Research shows that owning books is a key factor in holistic early development and lifelong academic and economic success: the effect of owning books outweighs a child's socio-economic status and is equaled only by parents' level of education! By working together to increase book ownership among young children, we could effectively disrupt a cycle of inequality for good.

Book Dash was established in 2014 by a group of publishers passionate about adapting publishing processes to be more inclusive, and thereby increasing access to beautiful, relevant books for all. The result was the Book Dash model: Skilled creative volunteers working in teams to create brand new, openly-licensed books in just one day. This innovative approach is estimated to save up to 80% of the costs usually associated with publishing new books, and that go on to make books prohibitively expensive to the vast majority of our population.

Since inception, Book Dash has worked with over 350 creatives who have volunteered their time and talent to create 156 original books at Book Dash events, hosted all over South Africa and now online too.

In addition to creating the books, we're passionate about mothertongue access and focus on facilitating South African language versions of our books. Currently, we have 550 language versions of Book Dash books available on the website. The full library is available free, for anyone anywhere to read, download, adapt, print or translate and we strongly encourage people to do so. The open license we use, Creative Commons CC BY 4.0 allows the books to travel widely: We know of over

a hundred cases of organisations and online free-reading platforms using and re-sharing the Book Dash books, taking our reach to millions of people daily, in the furthest reaches of the world. These adaptations range from tactile and South African Sign Language versions in South Africa to adaptations and translations in communities all over the world to increase access to diverse books in mothertongue. Publishers on the African continent are welcome to access the source files, and render and republish the books in local languages. The books are also featured and re-shared on the world's largest global digital libraries along with other reputable, award-winning open publishers for families and children to read and enjoy.

During the global pandemic, the number of people accessing the books on our website increased by 300%. We're thrilled that for many, our books provided a source of relief, bonding, stimulation and enjoyment even when centres of learning had to remain closed.

Increasing the number of books in a child's home is our vision. To date, with funding and distribution partnerships, we've printed and distributed almost 1.5 million physical books to children. We'd like to double that over the next two years, on our journey to a world where every child owns a hundred books by the age of five. We work with a network of over 200 trusted literacy and early childhood development organisations in South Africa, Lesotho and Eswatini to distribute the books to children and families to own, along with mediation in the form of training and activities to further encourage the essential early development that books can trigger.

Book Dash is humbled to have received numerous acknowledgements of our game-changing approach to equitable access to books for all young children. Over the years, we've been named winners at the South African Early Childhood Development Awards (2015), the Open Publishing Awards (2019), Community Chest Impumelelo Social Innovation Awards (2019) and recently we were the proud recipients of the 2020 Library of Congress Best Practice Honoree and the 2021 Nedbank Innovation Award.

Visit **bookdash.org** to find out more: read the books, download the source files, or find out how to host your own 12-hour book-making event following the Book Dash model.

Some of the mistakes that publishers can make

by Colleen Higgs

As publishers there are so many things that can go wrong in publishing a book. Especially during the production phase. Some of the mistakes are printer's mistakes, designer's mistakes, proofreader's and editor's mistakes, but as the publisher the buck stops with us. We have to take responsibility. We have to check at every single stage. In most jobs if you make a mistake it is between you and your boss or a client, but in publishing many of your mistakes can be public. Some of these mistakes can be very expensive, as you might have to withdraw the books from stores, then pulp and reprint. In the case of number 28, you might have to pay expensive legal fees.

Which of these have you made? Do you have any to add to the list?

1. Allocate a previously allocated ISBN to a new title
2. Allocate two ISBNS to the same title
3. Allocate the right ISBN but the book is printed with the incorrect barcode/ISBN so that the ISBN on the imprint page and the back of the book aren't the same
4. Random blank pages in the book
5. Spell the author's name incorrectly on the cover
6. tTypos
7. Have the book bound so that the pages fall out

8. Book can have sections wrongly bound together so page numbers are out of sequence
9. Printing not good enough, too light, pixellating happens
10. Book is bound so text is upside down to cover (first image)
11. Badly bound so it looks like a cat has eaten the book inside out
12. When printed the books are wavy, to do with glue not being dry before being packaged? Possibly.
13. Incorrect printer in imprint page
14. Don't notice that in printing all the lower case letter ds in italics are turned into a dot, because the software font used by the designer doesn't speak to the fonts that the printing software recognises. (second image).
15. Forget to acknowledge a donor
16. Not have wide enough inside margins (gutters) so you can't easily read the book
17. Spine incorrectly aligned

18. Spine not wide enough, so spine lettering bleeds over onto cover (third image)
19. Spine too wide
20. Spelling error on spine (fourth image)
21. Spelling error in blurb
22. Incorrect no of pages in catalogue or in BookData database
23. Publish a book that sales reps don't want to sub to bookstores because of the subjet matter (not really a mistake, but a challenge)
24. Print too many copies of a book, way too many
25. Budget according to an old specification that has now changed to a more expensive one
26. Think that if you go with a cheaper printer, the whole job will cost less
27. Think that if you go with a big, established printer that you will definitely get excellent service
28. Have to source an illustration for a picture book at the last minute because permission was denied or way too expensive for the image you intended to use.
29. Forget to ask for permission to use a quote, song lyric, image …
30. …

DigiThis – Meeting the Demands of Digital Becoming the New Normal
by Mark Hackney

While a great deal has happened over the last ten years in terms of the development of ebooks, and the ease of getting them to the consumer, developments in Africa seems to have been moving slowly. That is until the world and the way it works was turned upside down by the arrival of COVID-19.

The pandemic lockdowns have accelerated an already strong trend towards home entertainment with consumers staying home for safety and choosing sophisticated entertainment. This new normal of working and entertaining oneself at home has meant a surge in the purchase of electronic devices, laptops, and tablets. However, in Africa, none of these compares to the uptake of the smartphone over the last twelve-month period.

In South Africa, the growth in the use of smartphones was regarded as slow prior to 2014 where it was estimated that only 9.7 million people had smartphones. However, estimates are that this figure literally shot up to 24.5 million at the end of 2020, meaning that well over one third of the Country's population now have smartphones. This, coupled with cheap internet access that will soon be available in the country thanks to companies like FibrePoynt who are focused on providing high-speed internet solutions to low-income communities, should give authors and publishers an idea of South Africa's digital future, and the importance of getting onto an ebook platform.

THIS PAGE WAS GENEROUSLY SPONSORED BY RUTH HARTLEY

Where does all of this leave African authors and publishers in terms of the future of the ebook in Africa? While a comprehensive survey of the African ebook market is no doubt still deemed by many to be essential, it can be said that the prospects are starting to look good. Ebooks offer a low-risk option for authors that self-publish as fixed costs are lower, there are no inventory costs, nor are there any further costs if demand increases.

Overcoming the present barriers in terms of the scarcity of quality ebooks being produced in Africa should also not be deemed as impossible hurdles to overcome. Currently most ebooks are imported, which means high prices for the African consumer because of fluctuating exchange rates. DigiThis immediately provides an alternative for African authors and Publishers. Ebooks have the potential to offer so much more than a printed book. Both authors and publishers should benefit from sales of this valuable content and added value. It is for this reason that we at DigiThis have embarked on our new business model of ensuring that the authors and publishers are the major beneficiaries from the ebook retailing relationship.

Many African authors and publishers find themselves with their works being sold on ebook platforms where they have to relinquish a large percentage of their revenue or, alternatively, are subject to a confusing, complex, and convoluted payment system where admin, download and fulfilment fees are the order of the day. In response DigiThis offers an uncomplicated payment system where the author receives a far greater percentage of the proceeds for each sale, regardless of the price.

As a local and African ebook retail platform DigiThis believes in a jointly beneficial relationship between author, publisher, and e-retailer. Equally so they believe that for an author to succeed they must be allowed the flexibility to promote their books wherever they can and to be allowed to match market needs. For this reason, DigiThis operates on a non-exclusive basis and as such is a preferred alternative to the bigger ebook online retail platforms that take the greater percentage of the sales revenue. DigiThis appreciates the efforts that we need to make in actively marketing and promoting our clients' ebook titles. We also appreciate the importance of regular feedback to our clients so that we involve authors in customer relationships so they can make the most of those relationships.

Making use of simple to use ebook readers such as Adobe Digital Editions (ADE) and e-reading apps such as Bluefire Reader, customers can experience their ebook purchases in the most optimum format across PC, MAC, tablets, or mobile devices which can be read both online and offline. In addition, Bluefire Reader is deployed worldwide by leading brands in ebook retail, libraries, and academia. It is also the easiest, fastest, and most affordable way to launch apps on Apple iOS, Android, and Windows PCs.

At DigiThis we believe that simplicity in accessing digital materials is key for our customers as well as our authors and publishers. As such they will be ready for meeting digital becoming the new normal.

DigiThis is a subsidiary Books Direct, the Blue Weaver Marketing Online Retail Initiative.

For more information or to get your titles listed on Digi-This, please contact admin@booksdirect.co.za

The Africa Publishing Innovation Fund: an accelerant for African ingenuity

In 2019 the International Publishers Association (IPA) – the world's largest trade association for publishers – entered a partnership with UAE-based philanthropic organisation Dubai Cares to support literacy, book access, indigenous publishing, and library restoration in Africa.

Under the arrangement, Dubai Cares donates $200,000 a year for four years (2020-2024), and the IPA sponsors select African projects for maximum social impact. The IPA has entrusted the process to the Africa Publishing Innovation Fund Committee, which is chaired by IPA President, Bodour Al Qasimi, and comprises five other senior publishers from Ghana, Kenya, Nigeria, South Africa and Tunisia.

The APIF's two main focus areas are innovation in publishing and support for libraries, and the committee disburses funds annually according to the most urgent needs in those areas.

Details of APIF-sponsored projects can be found at **apinnovation.fund**

SUPPORTING AFRICAN LEARNING AMID COVID-19

Prompted by the COVID-19 pandemic, the APIF's 2021 grant cycle sought community-led innovations to keep students learning remotely and offer communities access to books and facilities for social cohesion, skills development, studying and reading.

THIS PAGE WAS GENEROUSLY SPONSORED BY TRACEY HAWTHORNE

School closures in 2020 sent governments scrambling to get more than 250 million students learning online almost overnight. Africa already had 100 million out-of-school children, and many African education systems and governments were unprepared for the move to homeschooling.

The IPA Africa Regional Seminars had previously highlighted how African educational systems are lagging in digital transformation and technology adoption, a situation compounded by insufficient spending on infrastructure, like libraries.

1. Keeping kids in the school system

There is evidence that children, especially girls, are at higher risk of dropping out of school during a pandemic. In Ghana, where just 70% children are reached by remote education, the APIF is supporting the Learners Girls Foundation (LGF) to keep 400 girls in rural communities learning. The project connects girls to tutors, mentors, role models and training programs aimed at increasing girls' enrollment in STEM fields.

LGF cofounder Kumuriwor Alira Bushiratu said, "Students transitioning to e-learning amid COVID-19 have faced so many setbacks, such as inadequate accessibility to network devices, poor network connections in rural areas, and cost of internet accessibility."

THIS PAGE WAS GENEROUSLY SPONSORED BY TRACEY HAWTHORNE

2. Supporting publishers, teachers, and librarians to shift online

Across Africa, the shift to remote learning has been complicated by a lack of accessible digital content, as evinced by the IPA's report From Response to Recovery: The Impact of COVID-19 on the Global Publishing Industry. Additionally, further studies show that many African teachers urgently need professional development and ongoing support to enable them to teach in the online space.

"Remote learning is more than providing lessons over the internet," said eKitabu CEO Will Clurman. "For teachers to fully embrace online teaching and learning, they need confidence to create, adapt and deliver content that is accessible and engaging for all learners."

To address these gaps, the APIF is supporting eKitabu in Kenya and Save the Children in Rwanda. Starting in Kenya, with plans to scale to 12 African countries, eKitabu will work with publishers to enrich remote learning for nine million students and teachers with accessible digital learning materials. For its part, Save the Children will train 270 librarians in eight community libraries, to strengthen reading culture in remote communities while providing digital reading materials in Kinyarwanda, to keep 1.6 million children reading while out of school.

3. Binding communities through libraries

More than mere book repositories, libraries are community centres for events, learning and accessing basic facilities. A recent UNESCO study found 89% of students lack computer access, implying how crucial libraries are for connectivity.

"Physical structures exist longterm and help develop the community through the range of learning opportunities that can happen there," said Samantha Thomas-Chuula, Head of Programs at Book Aid International on the importance of libraries in rural communities.

In Zanzibar, Book Aid International will use its APIF grant to transform three shipping containers into professionally staffed libraries. And in Zimbabwe, the APIF is sponsoring Chirikure Chirikure, the country's best-known poet, to create a library with a water source in the rural community of Nemashakwe, in Gutu district.

"With APIF's help we will install a solar power system at

the library, and hook up to the internet through a mobile network. The library will connect learners to information and become a center that connects and empowers the entire community," said Chirikure Chirikure.

Translating publishing ecosystem challenges into innovation

As the IPA has documented, publishers moved quickly to help school systems transition to online learning, fasttrack COVID-19 research, and provide an escape. The APIF-sponsored initiatives are a glimpse of the way publishers are innovating amid adversity, and testament to the value of publishing in working with teachers, libraries, governments, and civil society to innovate and turn adversity into opportunity.

Read. Write. African   *by Fébé Potgieter*
(Publisher: Khaloza Books)

For over a decade now, reports have shockingly revealed that 70% of South African children at a national level have difficulties learning to read (2011). This fundamental lack of a reading culture in South Africa ignited my passion to both encourage and contribute to the publishing space, particularly focusing on literature for children and young adults. The Progress in International Reading Literacy Study of 2016 confirmed that a whopping 78% of learners cannot "read for meaning by the age of 10." Two years later, the Statistics South Africa General Household Survey of 2018 showed that the problem starts even earlier; nearly half of parents or guardians of young pre-school children "never read books with children".

Since then a host of initiatives have started in South Africa to address this situation. There is the promise by Department of Basic Education to provide 1000 school libraries in five years, to the Equal Education Campaign for School Libraries. Then there are the awareness campaigns such as National Book Week in September each year, run by the South African Book Development Council and the Department of Arts and Council. There are a host of programmes in schools to improve literacy and reading, and to empower teachers better in this pursuit.

One of the issues that these initiatives often acknowledge, is the problem of access to books, hence the push for school and community libraries. Children's books are particularly expensive and not easily available to the majority of South Africans. In contrast, go to any market, formal or informal shops in Addis Ababa, Ouagadougou, Cairo, Dakar, Lagos and Zanzibar, and you will find a plethora of stalls and street vendors selling second-hand books. Children's books by local publishers are in abundance and are relatively cheap. Sadly, most of these books never make it beyond their local borders, even if published in kiSwahili, English, Arabic or French. There simply doesn't seem to be a Pan African market for children's books, or rather a large enough drive towards it. Khaloza Books was established to publish books that are Pan African, accessible across the continent and globe, and always published in both English and an indigenous language of Africa. There have been challenges and successes; namely the dual English and indigenous language value that is in all our publications has been well received, yet the will and availability of funds to purchase books for children remains limited.

The internet and ebooks have made the cost of accessing children's books from Tunisia to Tanzania and other parts of the continent easier. And there are many innovative projects. An institution such as Puku assists to curate and promote southern African children's books, providing a virtual marketplace for books and publishers. Ethnikds is an online bookstore which specialises in sales of children's books, whilst also doing events with authors. Then there is Book Dash, who "believes that every child should own one hundred books by the age of five." They advance this goal by providing a platform of African storybooks, "which anyone can freely translate, print and distribute" for free.

We are always looking for existing publishers, spaces, and initiatives that we can collaborate with to ensure greater reach and impact, but this is not without its own limitations. Printing and distribution of books remains the highest expense for small publishers, oftentimes catering for bigger more established publishers dominating the market. Additionally, a culture of reading ebooks is even less popular, often due to a lack of access to the internet or devices and data to read from. To mitigate these hurdles, Khaloza Books launched a weekly 'African Kids Book Club & Yoga', where children anywhere can join virtually, have story reading, parents are provided with information on where they can source books, and encouraged to gradually start building their home libraries. Additionally, we launched a 'School Reading & Writing Programme', in Ekurhuleni where we have a book club intervention twice a week for 2 hours

KHALOZA
BOOKS

Read • Write • African

each day that is incorporated into the curriculum and supported by the school's English department. This initiative has been most rewarding for all parties involved, but naturally had to be put on hold due to the COVID-19 pandemic – we look forward to its resurrection once schools reopen.

The global push for diversity and representation has also spurred a demand for African representation in the genre of children's books. Increasingly, popular African children's books are branching out beyond the genre of folktales or stories about animals. The International Board on Books for Africa (IBBY) did an exhibition in 2006 of 84 books for Africa, by Africa – showcasing the diversity of quality books from the continent. The fact that we have not had such an exhibition, even virtually, since then doesn't mean that children and young adult fiction are not being published. It just means that we have not done enough to explore how we can create and build markets for African children's books. We do our part to showcase the diversity that exists through our weekly 'African Book Reviews' focused on African authored books for children and young adults.

We hope as African publishers and authors, that we can come together and form distribution channels for book exchanges, and see our bookstores filled with African literature, and not merely as small forgotten aisles or shelves.

NOTES

NOTES

NOTES

NOTES

Printed in the United States
by Baker & Taylor Publisher Services